T0001367

COUNTRY

SONGS

FOR

ALICE

Country Songs for Alice
Copyright © 2024 Emma Binder. All rights reserved.

ISBN: 978-1-961209-02-2 (paper), 978-1-961209-05-3 (eBook)

Cover and text designed by Allison O'Keefe

Cover art: "Truck driver [with cowboy boots sticking out of truck window], Vernon, Texas, 1949." Russell Lee (American, 1903–1986). Photograph courtesy of the George Eastman Museum. Every reasonable effort has been made to identify copyright; if there are errors or omissions, please contact Tupelo Press so that corrections can be addressed in any subsequent edition.

First paperback edition: March 2024

All rights reserved. Other than brief excerpts for reviews and commentaries, no part of this book may be reproduced by any means without permission of the publisher. Please address requests for reprint permission or for course-adoption discounts to:

Tupelo Press
P.O. Box 1767
North Adams, Massachusetts 01247
(413) 664-9611 / Fax: (413) 664-9711
editor@tupelopress.org / www.tupelopress.org

Tupelo Press is an award-winning independent literary press that publishes fine fiction, non-fiction, and poetry in books that are a joy to hold as well as read. Tupelo Press is a registered 501(c)(3) non-profit organization, and we rely on public support to carry out our mission of publishing extraordinary work that may be outside the realm of the large commercial publishers. Financial donations are welcome and are tax deductible.

TUPELO PRESS
SNOWBOUND CHAPBOOK AWARD WINNERS

Emma Binder, *Country Songs for Alice* — Selected by Hala Alyan

Matthew Gellman, *Night Logic* — Selected by Denise Duhamel

Eric Pankey, *The Future Perfect* — Selected by John Yau

Tyler Mills, *City Scattered* — Selected by Cole Swenson

Chad Bennett, *Artifact of a Bygone Era* — Selected by Eduardo C. Corral

Meg Wade, *Slick Like Dark* — Selected by Kristina Marie Darling

Matt Donovan, *Rapture & the Big Bam* — Selected by Lia Purpura

Allan Peterson, *Other Than They Seem* — Selected by Ruth Ellen Kocher

Chad Parmenter, *Weston's Unsent Letters to Modotti* — Selected by Kathleen Jesme

Deborah Flanagan, *Or, Gone* — Selected by Christopher Buckley

Anna George Meek, *Engraved* — Selected by Ellen Doré Watson

Kathleen Jesme, *Meridian* — Selected by Patricia Fargnoli

Brandon Som, *Babel's Moon* — Selected by Aimee Nezhukumatathil

Stacey Waite, *the lake has no saint* — Selected by Dana Levin

John Cross, *staring at the animal* — Selected by Gillian Conoley

Cecilia Woloch, *Narcissus* — Selected by Marie Howe

Joy Katz, *The Garden Room* — Selected by Lisa Russ Spaar

Mark Yakich, *The Making of Collateral Beauty* — Selected by Mary Ruefle

David Hernandez, *A House Waiting for Music* — Selected by Ray Gonzalez

Barbara Tran, *In the Mynah Bird's Own Words* — Selected by Robert Wrigley

COUNTRY SONGS FOR ALICE

Emma Binder

THE FIRST SONG

If you want to come to my house, I'll let you in.
My house in the cold December desert. Metal shingles easing loose in snowstorms.
Right off the highway. We can listen and move in rhythm
with its traffic. I'll kick the kerosene lamp between my ribs,
unlock and loosen all my windows. *Which windows?* This wafer of glass
gloomed over with breath. Pane where the steam of cooked meat
beads into small, silver planets. The window between your thighs
which tinsels into thin air when asked the right question. If you want
to sit at my table, I'll spit-style my hair and serve you. I'll talk to you
with ripped silk in my throat, boiled creekwater, I'll track jackrabbits
all night through snow and drag them home. Boot-prints
have worn these soft floors into cotton. Lilac wafts in if you wait for it.
I'll slope into the dark for you. *Which window do you want to break?*
The iridescent sheen that divides the hurting bedroom
from the hurting wind. The smashed picture frame that sits beneath
a black leather saddle and a pinned rose, proof of boyhood. Alice,
if you knock, I'll hear chimes. Doesn't matter how deep asleep
I've been. The dream will cleave into two pieces, ruptured
by your name spelled out backwards in steam.

SONG

We'll wait in the truck stop parking lot for the sky's
                    gluey torches to catch. They'll call you a dyke. They'll call me

a dirty bitch. They don't know I'm not even
               a girl. They've never known the sensitive, angry texture
of your heart. They've never seen you coiled
                  against a bedspread, gold-cheeked
as if held to flame. Poor,

              dumb things. No way am I going home over some guy
leaning out his Chevy window who's never licked dust
                  off an angel's palm. He hasn't even slept
in meadows. He doesn't know

              about the washed knives of light in you. He can't hear
certain notes, like those slipped by mournful ghosts
                  into radio static, or the whimpers that dogs make
when they miss home. We'll padlock our names

              to the soot-stained fence around this lot.
We'll drive into that big-ass neon diner sign
                  if someone says we can't be here. We'll break
its letters into rhinestones of ice. *Are you ready?*

             Get in. Your eyelashes are haloed
in soft dirt and buckwheat. If this is a stage,
                  you're the actor who breaks plates,
burns the scenery. They don't deserve
              even to be burned by you.
But I'll follow your lead. You rogue, perfect trespasser.

SONG

You lived at your mom's house for a while, cooped up
in the dark carpeted room where she piled laundry. Green lights
from the garage narrowed into ribbons through the blinds.
We tracked dirt inside to make a more perfect world. We watched
the same movie over and over, listened to the same songs. *Weed, whites,
and wine.* Sweatshirts, denim, and spit. You cut my hair with a straight
razor left in the bathroom by your shithead dad. In a cloudy jar
on the windowsill, light shone through rubble from the moon. *I just
found this on the street*, you said, holding up a dirty black boot.
My eagle's head welded to your hooves. Your mom shouted
through the door: *Girls*, she called, *open up, I need my work clothes.*
Small, blonde meadows of hair came ablaze. Every dog
in the neighborhood shivered and skittered to its feet. In the months
ahead, I heard alarms: *Love isn't everything. Can't keep living
this way.* But your voice was milk. That carpeted room
was a furnace in a snowbound country. Little strands
of my black hair clung to your coiled sheets. *We're different*,
you said. So we played at mirroring one another. How close
could I get to you? How could the soft-finned animal of your hand
become mine? How many times could we raft through darkness
and survive? The moon rained down in sequins some nights.
When your mom knocked on the door, you put a hand on my mouth
to keep me quiet. The sounds that didn't leave me spun
into small, silver comets inside my chest.

SONG

I know there've been songs about horses but one
    is still unspooling from the mouth of this dusty-cheeked cowboy
who's singing, eyes closed, while hooves beat footpaths

    into the soft grasses of their voice. Every time they try to think
of their girl's freckled cheeks or schoolboy shirt, they see horses. Once they braked hard
    for a black horse with blue ingots inlaid deep

in its skull. Communing with those watery planets would take
    a lifetime of learned wisdom. Driving to her house tonight, they summon
the daring of horses. Is there a pageantry in the manes, tails, and riots

    of horses? The cowboy puts their queer hand to the horse's
snout. They named the horse Hot Grits but calls her Baby
    and Gorgeous. As in: *Hey Horse, you Sweet*

Rough and Tender Baby. They've heard all the ballads about what can't
    be tamed. On the other side of wilderness is the terror
they'll feel when it's over: raw grief, hooves pounding

    their heart, each midnight wider and blacker than the last. Always hurting
for that summer of horses, its dawn-soaked fields to which
    they can't return. Fording that kind of loss will take deftness, an ability

to handle their own fear. Rope skills. Deep knowledge of the woods
    around them. A talent for speaking to horses
with their hands, asking questions of the wild mane.

SONG

Alice you got cool blue stones in the reaches of your fingers.
    You can fix the truck. My hat's full of rain for you. I can count

on you to hop fences, stoke coals, rear the crooked sapling
    somebody left in a milk pail. You're a field

lit by a velvet couch on fire. The way you nurture doesn't mean
    you're not fierce. You can nurture me, feed me,

and bruise me in a breath. Your blue-gray bruises hide
    candlelight and sugar. In the dark,

steam-thickened cab of my truck, your palms glow like half-dollars.
    Moonlight rubs against a wick of hair,

then slides into a Styrofoam coffee cup and sits there. You know
    what to do. When the guy outside the bar

in Readstown moves like he'll kill us, you can burn a hole
    in his boot with that moonlight. You can

blind him for a fortnight. Cleave sidewalks
    with your salt-stained gloves. Birds will fly

backwards, eager to hunt mice and lay them
    at your feet. Soft red talon-marks

are proof that they love you, they listen to you, they're watching
    that light as it drips from your hair. They hover

as they wait to see what you'll do. I'm hovering,
    too. In the glovebox there's railroad

spikes, candy, and crumpled maps. You toss your light
    out the window. When the guy outside the bar

raises his fist, it's like a matchstick lost
        to prairie fire. We hardly even see it,
            amidst all that flame.

DIRT SONG

Deep dirt, paydirt. Cracked & battered
dry dirt. Dirt where a creek used to cleave
this valley into pieces. Dirt stitching creeks
into my palms and upper lip. How the pale,
silken hair on your forearms looks like sawgrass
in dirt. We *love* to get down in the dirt, F. said to me.
That's how come we all got to be friends.
Stray dirt finds its way into the trailer. You mimic
how lizards root through dirt with their tongues.
Cheap & foul dirt for blood. No marrow
in these bones but metal-tinseled, muddy-rich
dirt. All the prayers I scattered were for me,
the Earth, Alice, and my dirt-blooded family.
For God, the Angel, the Fire, and the
dirty-mouthed Truckdriver in me. If we hit dirt
in my Ranger, we might have to chain it
to H.'s truck. If you taste dirt, you might learn
what's apt to grow there. You got dirt in your teeth.
Nothing wrong with it — on the contrary.
How'd you learn to handle dirt that way?
Like bread and the satin ears of rabbits,
at the same time. Out of which you coax
the brightest saplings, jeweled tomatoes.
It's dirt wisdom. Dirt language.
You're talking, I've got my ear to the ground.

SONG

For years I was obsessed
    with rodeo. It had to do with rhythm:

bootprints on wooden,
    age-silvered bleachers. The slow,

gnostic orbit of dust
    like scripture. The jackknifing

cowboy's hips against his bronco.
    All of it sensual. But overlaid by fast,

dirty jokes and manure. Sweat and dust
    thickened into gum

around my temples. There was so much muscle
    bucking in that arena, no one much

looked at me. If I wore
    leather boots, flannel,

and denim, I was every
    other person. When really

I was a steer, broad-shouldered
    and comet-eyed. Muscled in my blood-

stained garments and quiet rage.
    My pulse quickened

with the secret joy
    of deceit. *They think I belong*

here. They think I'm tame. I loved
    to get away with it. Cloaked,

bonneted, and masked. Shielding
    my true nature like a lit match

inside a fist. Every part of me sacred. Even
    the fact that for years, only I knew

what I was. In the crowded stands
    I clenched my hand

around my secret flame and winced,
    as if bitten.

SONG

E. says, *I like the way those old guys*
talk. It's like music. Some who live alone

talk slow, like the thawed sap of a river
coming loose. Their water is deliberate,

learning its own driven flesh again,
finding its path after many weeks

among only wind and acreage.
There are other old ways: some people stand

in the middle of the road and won't leave
until the story's over or it rains. Some people

polish their family's bones
as they talk, rubbing the shapes

they inherited and don't understand.
Why these flattened vowels?

Why this twitch of the vocal chord,
this habit of twirling hair? Some people

weave braids or bird's nests
while they talk, but you won't realize

until you've walked away. Some people
are trying to tell you something.

Some people sow seeds in the expectation
that they'll know you and care for you

for years, so it doesn't need to all come out
at once. Some people, when they talk,

are dancing in the schoolyard between
what's heavy and light, dead and alive.

Some people seem to talk in circles, which,
to an unwitting ear, might look like repetition.

But every time they return to the same ground,
their bootprints sink deeper and the shape

of their path becomes script. Details
knock loose: little pink stones, bones

of lizards, bullet casings, a nail
you can use. These are useful

people. They'll come to you with pockets
full of unearthed tokens that they found

while treading the same places, trying
to understand what's buried

and what wants to get found.

SONG

It looks like there's nothing out there, F. says,
but there are little things. We're looking at the northern
Utah horizon, toward an oil drum half-eaten
by dirt and sun-bleached scrub. I know what she means.

There are tawny lizards and foxes. There are rusted
metal pails, squashed flat into coins. You think there's just
room and room, but you'll find billboard shrapnel and soup cans
with rusty mouths. The road where you talk

to yourself. A white crust on your lips. Tattered flags.
The wispy shadow of a flag that you mistake for smoke.
The footprints of a man who keeps following you. Marbles
of amber from the joints of an injured tree, blown in

from Castle Valley. The road where you wonder
who to call if you can't call your mother. Road maps
and groceries and plywood, slipped loose from truck beds.
Rocks chewed to bits by storms you almost died in. All the storms
you almost died in, still churning and waiting

for their chance to pounce back into your life. The road
where you remember what you forgot
to mention. The fact that what you didn't mention
looms large, scrawled across the horizon like a message

for the airplanes. The airstrip that tumbles
into nature. Nature falling back and fighting back
and getting strong and giving up again. The road
where you try to sort yourself out. If only you walk that road

every day, you think, you'll be fine to live with.
Snakes in their cool, private parlors. A road you haven't seen
but still dream about. A sign torn to lace with bullet holes.
A sign for a dead town outlasted by its bones.

SONG

We're standing on a plywood watchtower.
　　No guns. Not hunting.

　　　　Just watching the storm lumber in.

Alice looks like she belongs here.
　　Her dress is all blurry and bruise-colored,
like a cloud-eaten moon. The birds

　　　　still weave in and out,
playing with the storm's scribbled
　　lightning, playing

　　　　　to get caught.

Once I said, *I don't care if I get hurt.*
　　Burn up in a temple of flame and never
　　　　recover.

　　　But what did you mean?
What did you know about burning?
　　　The birds seem to crave that lightning,

　　　　its white, searing signature of pain.

SONG

I had one good summer of horses,
    which is more than some people get.

Joy in my dirty suntan and river-
    greased hair. I shut one eye to squint at Alice,
perched on her muck-slick rock

like a watchful bird. She was staring
    at the water and its rocks like pink and green

baubles. When an orb of sun slid past her,
    she seemed to transfigure. She was a deadly wind,
then a statue. She was the legs of horses

or a lion. Pear tree, nightmare,
    froth on the undersides of slate-blue

clouds. Then she returned, stood up,
    and leap-frogged back to me. Later,
I would curse the memory of what I'd seen

and would never see again. The only balm
    for anything is that you can sing about it,

G. said. Which is a shallow comfort
    when I visit that river alone.

SONG

One night I clutched you
like the wily mane of a nightmare.
Moonlight wetted stormclouds,

waxed your cheeks cold and blue.
We were in the backseat while E.
drove us to the store for propane

and water. Deer dashed
into the road like they wanted
to die. I could see your longing

as you watched the plains unfurling
backward. I didn't yet know
what you wanted. *You miss somebody?*

I asked. *Sure,* you said,
everybody. Then we arrived in town.
There was nobody around

except the through-hiker
who lived in her van. She was parked
outside the Sunoco, crouching

in only a thin jacket to charge her phone
by the vending machine. *Van's dead,*
she said to us. Then she started to cry.

You went to hold her
with a tenderness I hadn't seen
in months. We led the hiker

to E.'s truck. I sat up front
so you could sit with her.
I knew she needed warmth,

a shoulder and a cigarette,
but I was jealous. Jealousy
does nothing. It sits inside of you,

deadening the body like coal.
My goblet brimmed with coal
and I was starving. The billboards

we passed depicted pick-your-own
apples and grapes, magnolia
leaves of bounty. I get it,

I wanted to say. Fruits jeweled
and lavender. Juice dripping
like blood from your cheek. Even

the smallest cup, a thimble-full,
would slake me, but I starved
all the way home, catching glimpses

of your hand against the hiker's
thigh. My need for you was beginning
to poison me. I wanted

to go back but it was too late.
I wanted to rewind that tape
and live something else.

SONG

Dear Alice,
        Sometimes out here I catch sight
        of columns of smoke before the wind chips them
        into stairs. Sometimes the water
        tastes like cooked flowers. The chicken coop
        was full of snakes this morning. When it rains,
        I hear droplets hiss into steam as they hit
        my Ranger's roof. I get the sense that if I changed
        my name, no one would much care. Something in the throat
        gutters loose, gets free. With no one around
        you can be anything: animal, mineral,
        cloud pattern, blade. If only you could see me
        like this. Just yesterday I mopped blood
        with a piece of bread. After so much trouble
        with the body and what it signals, the world
        is suddenly content to leave me alone. Do I want
        to be left alone? In this condition? Do you still dream
        of motels and lit matches wafting above your bed?
        When I picture your new home, I imagine you
        sifting through tumbleweeds in bare ankles.
        The thorns that cut me don't cut you.
        Rain doesn't come until you knock on its dark door,
        demanding to be given what you came for.

SONG

Alice is everybody's brakelights. Always a good time
but already leaving. You can't make her stay,

G. said. You can't pin a twig of light to the window.
But you also can't forget what you felt: palmful

of yellow dress. The rarity of breath against
your ankle. Some days, despite it, there's enough

to distract you. You have your water chores,
your dust chores, your propane and brushfire

chores. The sun's a medallion but it doesn't
make any big reports. The animals, too,

say nothing. There are no horses
racing valiant inside you but you're not aching

over the thumbprints of dead stars, either.
Then you find yourself standing

someplace ordinary. You're in your truck or the Sunoco,
getting cussed out by the woman

who always cusses you out. You're in the middle
of the road, lifting a bloody fox

from the dotted line. Its one gray eye rolls forth
and begins speaking. Do you remember

her jaw, how you cupped it in your palm
like a flower bulb? Pale hair,

chipped teeth. These small details hurt you
the most. Before you knew her, Alice

was a blazing, distant torch on the horizon,
but one of many. Beautiful,

you might have said. Luminous.
Now you have details.

They're terrible. The fox's chest
has been steamed open. You can lift

her purple heart like a soft,
stewed apple. You eat the apple in hopes

that the fox will go quiet, but she doesn't.
Big surprise. In fact, now those bitter words

are inside you. The apple is laced
with tinsel-scars of metal. All the details

you've been cursed to remember
are floating upward like ghosts

from a bog. How she threw her arms
around B. when she met him.

The tenor of her voice that told you
she was looking elsewhere. The exact place

you were standing when you realized
that she could tire of you. She could tire

easily. The truck hood's heat
against your back as she stood before you,

in a moment so simple and still
until she said, *Maybe I'll move down South,*

where no one knows me. You almost asked
if you could come with but you knew

what she'd say. So you turned
your face away. You're still turning.

Now the sun is telling you
to lie down in the road. Just get

down. Hold the ravaged fox
to your chest, stop looking for her.

The apple inside you
is talking. It won't stop talking

until you forfeit yourself to the road.
It's louder than anything, even

the highway wind. Which whips past like
horses stampeding toward mountains.

But there are no horses to be seen.

SONG

I could be cavalier about the desert's hazards.
    It wasn't just thirst. Not just isolation, either.

A man in a bucket hat drove his flatbed
    in circles with a rifle perched lengthwise
across his knees. E. told me a story

    about a wind-torn gate that slipped into an open
car window and severed the driver's head.

    His partner was in the passenger seat.
No one knew how he stopped the car,
    or how he kept breathing. Sometimes when I walk

across the plains on a windless day, I think about
    all the places where people have been torn

from this earth before they were prepared. How those places
    are scorched by pinched stars. They whiten the soft dirt,
and everything that grows from the stars is bloodless. People

    come here seeking sanctuary,
aloneness. If you try, you can walk among those white wounds

    in the earth as if they were roses. *It will never happen
to me* is the song you sing to yourself
    as the man drives past, so slowly you can almost

hear the tick of his heart.

SONG

There are roots in the plains, but you have to dig deep. You need hooves or adaptations, like how the fox twists her shadow into scrap metal, to camouflage herself from hunters in their cars. When the wind dies down, you can smell purple bulbs and hidden agate. That's how you'll know the animal parts of you are not dead. You must sleep in your truck. Sweat through the awful dream. Pinch the moonlight off your legs like a bedsheet. Wrap yourself in your taking-out-the-garbage coat, green and stained and coarse, from Army Surplus. In the middle of the night, all the eyes of nocturnal creatures will twitch like candles. Shake the ants from your black hair, watch stubble sprout on your stomach and chin. Such wildness has to it the tinny cast of a nightmare. But it's a nightmare to which you belong. Climb out of the truck bed and burrow, with the snakes, for cool blue roots that tie land together. There are no bits of property. Just this impermeable, secret net. The raw pulse of that net is alive in your hands, skipping like a heartbeat. That's something you get to keep forever. That feeling.

THE LAST SONG

There came an era of endless parties at H.'s place.
An era when I did nothing but weigh different ways to die. An era
of sitting on my tailgate in the Cinemark parking lot,

where you worked one summer, scrubbing scorched black butter
from the popcorn machine. Then an era of silence. I know
I'm moving quick. But I'm trying to get it all down

before the next phone call, the next curl of thunder that unlaces me.
Because then I'll have to start over. An era of cowpokes
and greasy fries. An era of barbecue. An era when I told everyone

I didn't miss you. I kept saying that: *I don't even miss her. I don't even*
think about her. I don't even dream about her. I don't even dream. An era
of charred matchsticks, burnt brush. An era of buzzed hair

and night sweats. Streamers of twilight crept into my bedsheets.
Until dawn I planned how I would drive into the river
in my truck full of cracked cassettes and tin cans, spare clothes

from that month when I had no place to go. I punched
the thin pane between my bedroom and the wind. Whenever someone
said your name, I turned my face. I made a joke. I said something like,

No thanks, I've had plenty. Even though I would have eaten at your table,
I would have gnawed red stars and cried like a dog. I would have loosed
my floodlights on your lawn. I would have eaten fistfuls of dirt

or walked into the train tunnel's black socket, from which some people
never get to walk out. There came an era of pig bones and ash-speckled
snow. My coveralls were caked with shiny blood

from where I'd been the previous night, but couldn't
remember. Half the time I looked up and found a windshield,
but had no knowledge of how I'd gotten there,

or which town I was in. I wanted to drink all day and night
until my mouth burned. Until cornflowers flamed blue
in my memory. I wanted to drive through the rain,

even when my friends begged me to turn around. K. made me eggs
and coffee to keep me upright. G. let me sleep on their floor.
The steam-engine in me, a dollop of fire, kept pressing me

to the wheel. Then came an era of dregs, boozy tar,
fender on the asphalt fanning sparks like water. Then came the era
of gold embers, whittled into threads by bare wind. But I stayed

awake. I put my palm to the battered road. I wept at the glint
of headlights on chickenwire. I laid awake wrestling with my handfuls
of storm. I couldn't stop dreaming of your face, lit gold from the inside

like a paper moon. I couldn't stop shoveling up
old pain. I stood solitary on a desert road, where rain rattled me
like dice in a tin can, where the elbows in my shirt went threadbare

with weather. I couldn't drive past a field of mangy horses
without feeling like I'd been slapped. Something about
their great bony skulls, thrown back against the pageantry

of wind, upended me. And then I'd go back
to my truck and wage tiny, inconsequential battles
against my heartbeat, the road, the sprawling night.

It all feels smaller now. I understand that country songs
are meant to describe a feeling, at most a chapter,
because you can't live your life

while you're hurting and drinking that way. I had to
wake up to the sky's excoriating blueness, that sunlight
that seemed to carve me down to my livid bones.

I had to make a decision. I had to drop my keys
in a lake. But sometimes I still want to ride out with my hands
on your shirttail, while coyotes howl in a wind-tipped

chorus. I still want to watch twilight churn
from a technicolor chord into a staircase. The feeling comes
at night. It makes me want to drive west, seeking daybreak,

and speed fast into a sun that isn't sun, but stained glass.

ACKNOWLEDGMENTS

Thank you to *The Texas Review*, where the poems "[We'll wait in the truck stop parking lot…]," "[You lived at your mom's house…]," and "[Alice you got cool blue stones…]" previously appeared.

Thank you to Eileen Muza, Rema, and the Home of the Brave Residency in Cisco, Utah, where in May 2021 I finished these poems and felt deeply inspired and alive. I'm also deeply grateful for everyone I met while staying in Cisco, a desert sanctuary for fellow queers, freaks, and wanderers, some of whom heard me read these poems on an old Camaro under a full moon. You all made me feel at home. Cisco forever.

Deepest thank you to the original Western Mass Workshop, who read the earliest iterations of *Country Songs for Alice*: Hank Brakeley, Nico Gomez-Horton, Connor Grogan, Jake Klar, Greg McCarthy, Jo O'Lone-Hahn, Nellie Prior, and Ben Socolofsky. Thank you for the notes and the long nights and the love. I don't know what kind of writer I'd be if I didn't get to have workshops with my friends in kitchens, porches, backyards, and living rooms. This book is for you.

Thank you to my parents and siblings. And thank you to Frances Jane Sleger, for everything.

Lastly, thank you to all the people who sing good country music. I just don't know where I'd be.

ABOUT THE AUTHOR

Emma Binder is a writer from Wisconsin. They received their MFA from the University of Wisconsin, Madison, and were the 2020–2021 Hoffman-Halls Emerging Artist Fellow at the Wisconsin Institute for Creative Writing. They received the 2023 Indiana Review Fiction Prize, the 2022 Gulf Coast Prize in Fiction, and the 2022 Tupelo Press Snowbound Chapbook Award. Their work has appeared or is forthcoming in *The Kenyon Review*, *Gulf Coast*, *The Indiana Review*, *Pleiades*, *Narrative*, *The Texas Review*, *DIAGRAM*, and elsewhere.